THE GREAT DEPRESSION WASN'T ALWAYS SAD!

ENTERTAINMENT AND JAZZ

MUSIC BOOK FOR KIDS

Children's Arts, Music & Photography Books

BABY PROFESSOR
EDUCATION KIDS

Speedy Publishing LLC
40 E. Main St. #1156
Newark, DE 19711
www.speedypublishing.com

In this book, we're going to talk about entertainment and jazz music during the Great Depression. So, let's get right to it!

Soon after the 1929 Stock Market crash, the Great Depression started. It was a time of intense economic hardship for most Americans. Luxury items were a thing of the past. Many people, over 30% of the population, were out of work and standing in soup lines to get enough to eat. For most of the population, spending money on entertainment of any type was out of the question.

Great Depression Unemployed Men 1930's

However, during difficult times, entertainment is important because it lifts people's spirits and helps them dream of a better future.

One form of entertainment that helped people get through the Great Depression was music. Because music was widely available via radio, it was accessible to almost everyone. Music had always been very popular, but during the 1930s it became even more popular as a way to escape day-to-day hardships.

African American man playing piano in darkness.

JAZZ MUSIC
IN THE 1930s

Artist Roman Nogin painting series "Sounds of Jazz."

New Orleans, Louisiana was the place where jazz music was born. After the first World War, a large group of jazz musicians traveled north to New York and Chicago to earn a living. This changed the landscape of jazz music as each city molded its own unique style.

Man playing guitar.

The came the 1920s, and Prohibition from 1920 to 1933, a time when alcohol was banned throughout the United States. Jazz became the music of choice in speakeasies, which were nightclubs that sold alcohol illegally.

Jazz trumpet player.

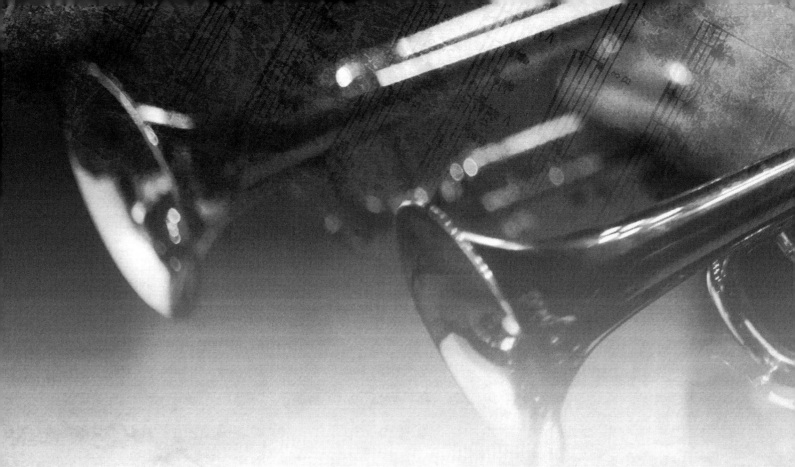

The spread of jazz was helped along by more advanced devices for recording. In a very short time, jazz music went from a regional style of music to being accepted and popular with the masses. Cab Calloway who was an African-

Trumpets in the hands of the musicians

American jazz singer at the Cotton Club in the neighborhood of Harlem, New York and Chick Webb, who was an African-American jazz and swing bandleader, were two of the many stars that became famous during this era.

Jazz Clubs on 52nd Street, New York, N.Y.

Unfortunately, there was still a great deal of racial prejudice so African-American musicians didn't get as much radio airtime as white musicians. Despite this, many African-American musicians were still discovered by listeners in clubs, ballrooms, and on the air.

Here are just a few of the great African-American and Creole jazz musicians of that era:

- **LOUIS ARMSTRONG**, a jazz trumpeter, singer, and composer

- **JELLY ROLL MORTON**, ragtime and jazz pianist

Trumpeter, bandleader and singer Louis Armstrong.

- **JOE "KING" OLIVER**, jazz cornet player and bandleader

- **FLETCHER HENDERSON**, jazz and swing pianist and composer

- **DUKE ELLINGTON**, pianist, big-band leader, and composer

Jazz musician Duke Ellington.

RADIO DAYS

Radio broadcasts had entertained American families since the 1920s. In the 1930s, radio programming had a *"Golden Age."* Radio became an entertainment lifeline for people as they gathered around in the evening to listen to music and different types of radio shows. It was a comfortable way to try out new types of music and comedy from the comfort of their familiar living rooms.

Talk Radio Announcer

A popular form of radio show was the *"Potter Palm."* This was an on-the-air amateur musical performance of big-band artists that was broadcast from Chicago or New York.

There was a type of program for every type of listener. News, theatrical performances, soap operas, Christian sermons, and musical shows were all popular.

Funny radio show on air. CANINE CODE.

Beginning in 1933, President Franklin D. Roosevelt used the radio to his advantage by broadcasting on national channels. His *"Fireside Chats"* kept the American people informed and inspired during the height of the Great Depression.

Radio Time

Amos 'n' *Andy,* a radio comedy with two main African-American characters that were voiced by white men gained over 40 million listeners around 1930. It was controversial because of the way black characters were portrayed. In 1938, Abbott and Costello, another famous comedy duo, were introduced on *The Kate Smith Hour.*

George Burns and Gracie Allen, a married couple in real life, began their hugely successful comedy careers first in vaudeville and then on radio.

Man listening to radio

There were also mystery shows like *The Shadow*, which, for a time, was voiced by Orson Welles, and adventure shows like *The Lone Ranger*.

With his warm baritone singing voice, Bing Crosby became a popular vocalist in the 1930s and so did Gene Autry, the ballad-singing cowboy. Another form of music that became known by mainstream audiences during the 1930s was country music.

The Grand Ole Opry radio program was started in November of 1925 and its *"Barn Dance"* music broadcast from Nashville became very popular during the 1930s. Country, gospel, folk, and bluegrass music were featured and there were also short comedy skits.

Man with baby in speaker horn of an old radio.

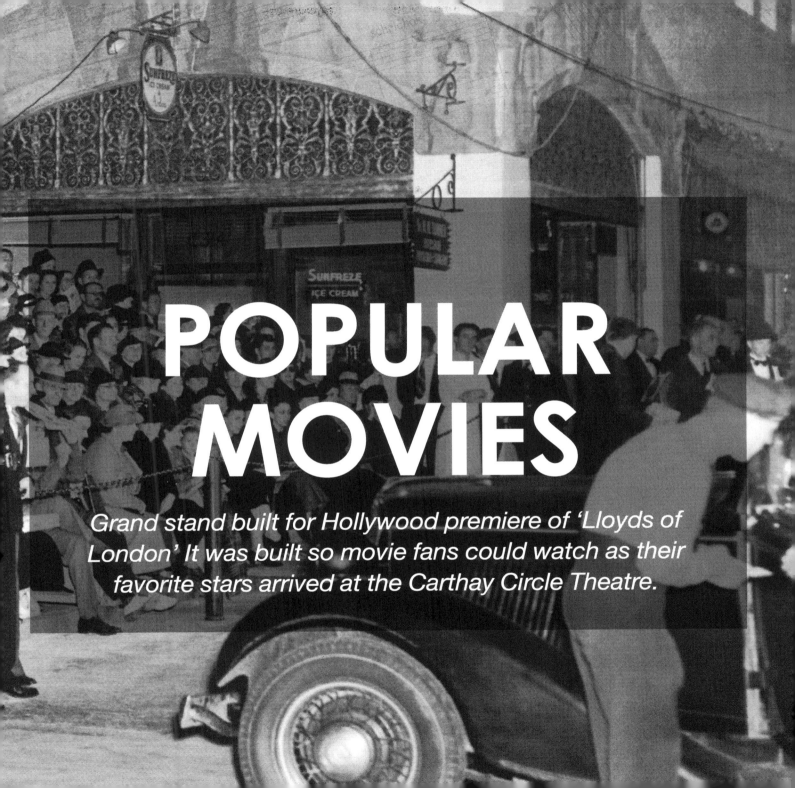

POPULAR MOVIES

Grand stand built for Hollywood premiere of 'Lloyds of London' It was built so movie fans could watch as their favorite stars arrived at the Carthay Circle Theatre.

By the 1930s, the silent films of the 1920s had given way to *"talkies."* Films were being made both in black and white as well as full color. The Big Five studios controlled the movie theaters and the process of movie making. The executives realized that people wanted to escape the hardship of their Depression-era lives so they concentrated on fantasy films that would distract people from their troubles for an hour or two.

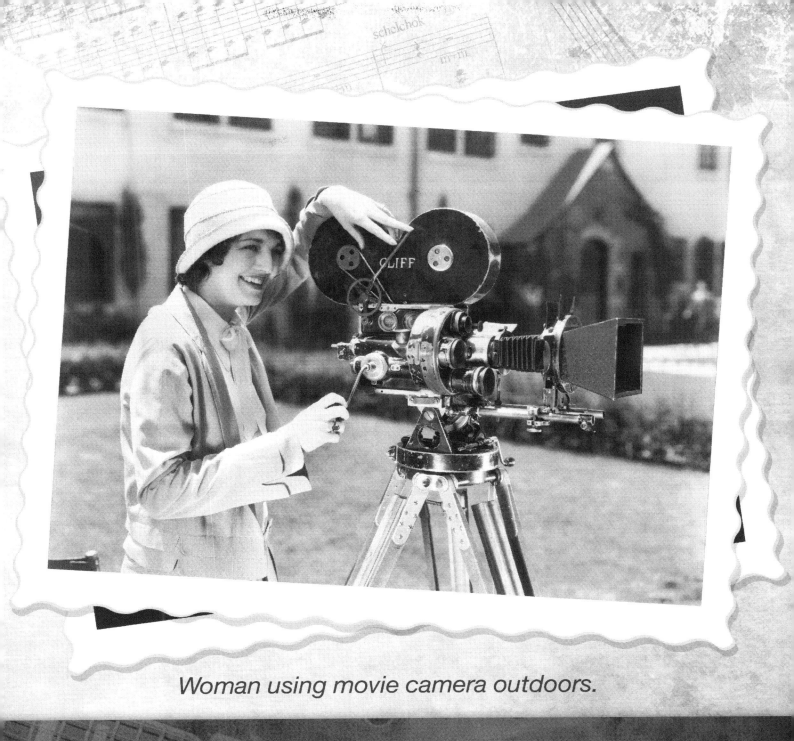

Woman using movie camera outdoors.

CARL LAEMMLE presents
FRANKENSTEIN
THE MAN WHO MADE A MONSTER
with
COLIN CLIVE, MAE CLARKE, JOHN BOLES, BORIS KARLOFF, DWIGHT FRYE, EDW. VAN SLOAN & FREDERIC KERR
Based upon the Mary Wollstonecraft Shelley Story
Adapted by John L. Balderston from the play by Peggy Webling
DIRECTED BY JAMES WHALE
A UNIVERSAL PICTURE
PRODUCED BY CARL LAEMMLE, JR.

Some of these films have stood the test of time and are still popular today. Monster films, such as *Frankenstein* and also *Dracula,* both made in 1931, and *King Kong* made in 1933 were very popular. One of the best films of 1939, *The Wizard of Oz* from the bestselling book by L. Frank Baum is still loved today.

Poster from the 1931 film Frankenstein.

Romantic films, such as *It Happened One Night* made in 1934, and *Gone with the Wind* made in 1939, both starring Clark Gable, were swooned over by women desperate for romance. Alfred Hitchcock's *The 39 Steps* made in 1935 by a British film company and *Mutiny on the Bounty* made the same year provided drama and intrigue.

"The Mummy" theatrical release poster, 1932.

Charlie Chaplin in City Lights.

Just as comedies were popular on radio, they were popular in movie theaters as well. Charlie Chaplin, who was one of the biggest stars in the world during the thirties, was in silent comedies such as *City Lights* and *Modern Times,* which showed his character

Scene from the 1931 film Monkey Business.

called **"The Little Tramp"** making his way through the difficult times of the Depression. The madcap Marx Brothers also kept people laughing with their classic comedies *Monkey Business* made in 1931, *Horse Feathers* made in 1932, and *Duck Soup* made in 1933.

During this time, the Walt Disney studios started to emerge. Disney's character Mickey Mouse had starred in a short film called *Steamboat Willie* in 1928 and the American public fell in love with him. Mickey would eventually be the star in over 120 cartoon shorts. At the movie theaters in 1930, Disney introduced the Mickey Mouse Club. The club had over a million children as members by 1932.

Steamboat Willie

Snow White 1937 trailer screenshot.

In 1937, at the height of the Depression, Disney took an enormous risk when he and his studios created a full-length color animated film, *Snow White and the Seven Dwarfs*. People in the industry thought Disney was crazy to attempt this, and his expense for the film exceeded a million dollars. At that time, a movie ticket cost a little over a quarter and families flocked to see this amazing film that had been created with technology that the Walt Disney Studios had invented.

CONTESTS, BOARD GAMES AND MORE

One way that people were enticed to come to the movies was through contests. Their tickets would be entered to win a prize when they came to the theater. Another popular type of contest included a marathon of dancing. Dance couples would compete against each other to see who could remain on the dance floor for the longest time. Some of these competitions lasted for days until

Couples Swing Dancing

the remaining couples collapsed and there was just one winning couple left.

Neighborhood hosted Soapbox Derby.

Other crazy contests included a contest to see who could swallow the most live goldfish, kissing marathons to see who could hold a kiss for the longest period of time, sitting atop a flagpole for the longest period of time possible, and races where kids constructed their own racecars from crates and other inexpensive materials. These races were the beginning of soapbox derby races.

Board games were popular during the Depression because they offered inexpensive entertainment. One of the bestselling board games of all time, Monopoly, was created by the Parker Brothers and first sold in 1935. Ironically, the game is about attaining money, wealth, and real estate. Another innovation in the thirties was the electronic pinball machine. Miniature golf provided a fun way for families to spend an afternoon without breaking the bank.

Monopoly Game Piece

Seven of the American League's 1937 All-Star players, from left to right Lou Gehrig, Joe Cronin, Bill Dickey, Joe DiMaggio, Charlie Gehringer, Jimmie Foxx, and Hank Greenberg.

SPORTS

Baseball was at the height of its popularity during the Depression. Kids could play in the park for no charge and it wasn't too expensive to attend a professional game. The New York Yankees were the most famous of all the teams. Players like Babe Ruth, Lou Gehrig, and Joe DiMaggio became sports celebrities.

College football was very popular as well. The first Heisman Trophy was awarded in the year 1935. New bowl games were played as well, such as the Orange Bowl and the Sugar Bowl.

Football Players

Awesome! Now you know more about entertainment during the Great Depression. You can find more Art, Music, & Photography books from Baby Professor by searching the website of your favorite book retailer.

Jazz guitarists hands.